Quotes for All the Feels

SHAWN CORNELIUS

Published by Yukon Publishing
Strongsville, Ohio
www.yukonpublishing.com

Copyright © 2025 Shawn Cornelius
All rights reserved.

ISBN-13: 978-0-9982672-3-4

DEDICATION

To my son, Matthew,
whose intellectual curiosity keeps my mind sharp
and whose emotional capacity keeps my heart full.

CONTENTS

Introduction 7
Angry Feelings 11
   When you are feeling Angry 12
   When you are feeling Annoyed 16
   When you are feeling Bitter 20
   When you are feeling Criticized 24
   When you are feeling Cynical 28
   When you are feeling Discouraged 32
   When you are feeling Disrespected 36
   When you are feeling Frustrated 40
   When you are feeling Hateful 44
   When you are feeling Jealous 48
   When you are feeling Judgmental 52
   When you are feeling Pessimistic 56
   When you are feeling Resentful 60
   When you are feeling Vindictive 64
Empty Feelings 69
   When you are feeling Apathetic 70
   When you are feeling Discontented 74
   When you are feeling Disillusioned 78
   When you are feeling Hopeless 82
   When you are feeling a sense of Longing 86
   When you are feeling Lost 90
   When you are feeling Nostalgic 94
   When you are feeling Sensitive 98
   When you are feeling Vulnerable 102
   When you are feeling Withdrawn 106
Fearful Feelings 109
   When you are feeling Afraid 110
   When you are feeling Apprehensive 114
   When you are feeling Helpless 118
   When you are feeling Inadequate 122
   When you are feeling Indecisive 126

- When you are feeling Insecure **130**
- When you are feeling Rejected **134**
- When you are feeling Self-Conscious **138**
- When you are feeling Weak **142**
- When you are feeling Worried **146**
- When you are feeling Worthless **150**

Sad Feelings **155**

- When you are feeling Disappointed **156**
- When you are feeling Embarrassed **160**
- When you are feeling Heartbroken **164**
- When you are feeling Hurt **168**
- When you are feeling Let Down **172**
- When you are feeling Like a Failure **176**
- When you are feeling Lonely **180**
- When you are feeling Regretful **184**
- When you are feeling Sad **188**

Stressed Feelings **193**

- When you are feeling Anxious **194**
- When you are feeling Burned Out **198**
- When you are feeling Confused **202**
- When you are feeling Impatient **206**
- When you are feeling Overwhelmed **210**
- When you are feeling Stressed **214**
- When you are feeling Under Pressure **218**

Tired Feelings **221**

- When you are feeling Bored **222**
- When you are feeling Exhausted **226**
- When you are feeling Stagnant **230**
- When you are feeling Stuck **234**
- When you are having Trouble Starting **238**
- When you are feeling Unfocused **242**
- When you are feeling Uninspired **246**
- When you are feeling Unmotivated **250**

Acknowledgements **255**
Author Index **256**

Quotes for All the Feels

INTRODUCTION

"Words are, in my not-so-humble opinion, our most inexhaustible source of magic. Capable of both inflicting injury and remedying it."

– Dumbledore, played by Michael Gambon
"Harry Potter and the Deathly Hollows, Part 2"
Directed by David Yates
Warner Bros.

I have always loved a great quotation. There is something truly special about how the perfect quote can concisely and elegantly capture a feeling or impart wisdom.

A great quote isn't just read or heard, it is **felt**.

In doing my research for this book I was disappointed with what was already available in the way of quotation books or sites on the Internet. They mostly read as flat lists of quotes, disconnected from the emotional state of the reader, effectively ruining the magic. They also often consisted of far too many or far too few quotes across a limited set of sources.

I am hopeful that you will find this book to be unique in its organization and in the variety of sources. There are 459 quotes in this book; organized across 59 different feelings; sourced from ancient philosophers, modern social media influencers, and everything in-between; and including genres across philosophy, literature, politics, movies, television, social media, music, and more.

Not all quotes will speak to you at a given time – if not then move to the next one, but I encourage you to feel the quote, don't just read it.

If you love a great quote, feel free to read this book cover-to-cover. Otherwise, I recommend you use this book as an emotional reference, by first identifying how you are feeling and then reading the relevant quotes for that chapter.

Often we may have the "feels" but not be able to quite identify what emotion we're really feeling. To help, I've included a "Table of Feels" on the opposite page, that mirrors the table of contents. Use this table by first determining if your overarching feeling is one of Anger, Emptiness, Fear, Sadness, Stress, or Tiredness. Then you can drill down into a more specific emotion or even peruse that entire section of the book.

Angry	Empty	Fearful
Angry	Apathetic	Afraid
Annoyed	Discontented	Apprehensive
Bitter	Disillusioned	Helpless
Criticized	Hopeless	Inadequate
Cynical	Longing	Indecisive
Discouraged	Lost	Insecure
Disrespected	Nostalgic	Rejected
Frustrated	Sensitive	Self-Conscious
Hateful	Vulnerable	Weak
Jealous	Withdrawn	Worried
Judgmental	Worthless	
Pessimistic		
Resentful		
Vindictive		

Sad	Stressed	Tired
Disappointed	Anxious	Bored
Embarrassed	Burned Out	Exhausted
Heartbroken	Confused	Stagnant
Hurt	Impatient	Stuck
Let Down	Overwhelmed	Trouble Starting
Like a Failure	Stressed	Unfocused
Lonely	Under Pressure	Uninspired
Regretful		Unmotivated
Sad		

A few notes about the citing of quotations…

Given the nature of quotes, they are often repeated, tweaked, translated, abbreviated, and misattributed. As a result, there is sometimes a large amount of controversy and disagreement among experts around whom should be credited with the origination of a specific quote. Several websites (for example, quoteinvestigator.com) exist for the sole purpose of researching quote origins.

In order to most accurately represent the source of each quote, I performed my own research, and this book reflects the latest consensus on who should be credited.

If a quote is often misattributed in popular culture, I've included a note in the book calling out that misattribution, since you may have heard the quote before, attributed to a different individual. In fact, many quotes that are commonly reported to be from Mark Twain, Winston Churchill, or Aristotle are not from them at all. In the event that a quote cannot be sourced to an individual, for example because it's so common it appears to have always been in existence, it will be attributed in this book to "Anonymous."

Quotes also drift and evolve as modern language evolves, as they are translated across languages, or as they are shortened for brevity. In those cases, the popular modern version is included here, with a note that it is paraphrased from the original.

Lastly, if a quote is from a book, movie, song, or TV show, the source will be listed alongside the author. If it was spoken in an interview or just generally attributable to an individual, no specific literary source will be listed.

ANGRY FEELINGS

When you are feeling **Angry**

Get mad, then get over it.

– Colin Powell

Anybody can become angry – that is easy, but to be angry with the right person and to the right degree and at the right time and for the right purpose, and in the right way – that is not within everybody's power and is not easy.

– Aristotle

Holding on to anger is like grasping a hot coal with the intent of throwing it at someone else; you are the one who gets burned.

— Buddhaghoṣa (paraphrased)

Anger is an acid that can do more harm to the vessel in which it is stored than to anything on which it is poured.

— Anonymous
(often misattributed to Mark Twain)

How much more grievous are the consequences of anger than the causes of it.

— Marcus Aurelius

For every minute you remain angry, you give up sixty seconds of peace of mind.

— Anonymous
(often misattributed to Ralph Waldo Emerson)

Whatever is begun in anger ends in shame.

— Benjamin Franklin

He who angers you conquers you.

— Elizabeth Kenny

When you are feeling
Annoyed

Reacting in anger or annoyance will not advance one's ability to persuade.

– Ruth Bader Ginsburg

The mind is its own place, and in itself can make a heaven of hell, a hell of heaven.

– John Milton, "Paradise Lost"

We don't see things as they are, we see them as we are.

— Anais Nin, "Seduction of the Minotaur"

Everyone thinks of changing the world, but no one thinks of changing himself.

— Leo Tolstoy, "Three Methods of Reform"

There is nothing either good or bad, but thinking makes it so.

— William Shakespeare, "Hamlet"

If you want the rainbow, you gotta put up with the rain.

— Dolly Parton

The world as we have created it is a process of our thinking. It cannot be changed without changing our thinking.

– Albert Einstein

The future belongs to those who believe in the beauty of their dreams.

– Anonymous
(often misattributed to Eleanor Roosevelt)

When you are feeling **Bitter**

Bitterness is like cancer. It eats upon the host.

– Maya Angelou

Never cut a tree down in the wintertime. Never make a negative decision in the low time. Never make your most important decisions when you are in your worst moods. Wait. Be patient. The storm will pass. The spring will come.

– Robert H Schuller

Remember that complaining about a problem without proposing a solution is called 'whining.'

— Teddy Roosevelt

Don't go around saying the world owes you a living. The world owes you nothing. It was here first.

— Robert J. Burdette
(often misattributed to Mark Twain)

The secret of change is to focus all of your energy not on fighting the old, but on building the new.

— Dan Millman, "Way of the Peaceful Warrior"

Never succumb to the temptation of bitterness.

— Martin Luther King Jr.

If life gives you limes, make margaritas.

— Jimmy Buffett

People won't have time for you if you are always angry or complaining.

— Stephen Hawking

When you are feeling **Criticized**

It is not the critic who counts: not the man who points out how the strong man stumbles or where the doer of deeds could have done better. **The credit belongs to the man who is actually in the arena**, whose face is marred by dust and sweat and blood, who strives valiantly, who errs and comes up short again and again, because there is no effort without error or shortcoming, but who knows the great enthusiasms, the great devotions, who spends himself in a worthy cause; who, at the best, knows, in the end, the triumph of high achievement, and who, at the worst, if he fails, at least he fails while daring greatly, so that his place shall never be with those cold and timid souls who knew neither victory nor defeat.

– Theodore Roosevelt

Nothing can dim the light that shines from within.

— Maya Angelou

Stay away from those people who try to disparage your ambitions. Small minds will always do that, but great minds will give you a feeling that you can become great too.

— Mark Twain

You can't let praise or criticism get to you. It's a weakness to get caught up in either one.

– John Wooden

I like criticism. It makes you strong.

– Lebron James

Do what you feel in your heart to be right – for you'll be criticized anyway.

– Eleanor Roosevelt

The trouble with most of us is that we would rather be ruined by praise than saved by criticism.

– Norman Vincent Peale, "The Power of Positive Thinking"

When you are feeling **Cynical**

Cynicism masquerades as wisdom, but it's the furthest thing from it. Because cynics don't learn anything. Because cynicism is a self-imposed blindness: a rejection of the world because we are afraid it will hurt us or disappoint us. Cynics always say 'no.' But saying 'yes' begins things. Saying 'yes' is how things grow.

— Stephen Colbert

Cynicism, to me, is trying to make people as unhappy as you are.

– Ricky Gervais

Most cynics are really crushed romantics: they've been hurt, they're sensitive, and their cynicism is a shell that's protecting this tiny, dear part in them that's still alive.

– Jeff Bridges

A cynical young person is almost the saddest sight to see, because it means that he or she has gone from knowing nothing to believing nothing.

— Maya Angelou

We know that in tough times, cynicism is just another way to give up, and in the military, we consider cynicism or giving up simply as forms of cowardice.

— Jim Mattis

Watch what people are cynical about, and one can often discover what they lack.

– George S. Patton

Never doubt that a small group of thoughtful, committed, citizens can change the world. Indeed, it is the only thing that ever has.

– Margaret Mead

When you are feeling **Discouraged**

When everything seems to be going against you, remember that the airplane takes off against the wind, not with it.

— Henry Ford

One day, in retrospect, the years of struggle will strike you as the most beautiful.

— Sigmund Freud

Discouraged

It is a rough road that leads to the heights of greatness.

– Lucius Annaeus Seneca

It's supposed to be hard. If it wasn't hard, everyone would do it. The hard is what makes it great.

– Jimmy Dugan played by Tom Hanks
"A League of Their Own"
Directed by Penny Marshall
Columbia Pictures

If there is no struggle, there is no progress.

— Frederick Douglass

The flower that blooms in adversity is the rarest and most beautiful of all.

— The Emperor voiced by Pat Morita
"Mulan"
Directed by Barry Cook and Tony Bancroft
Walt Disney Company

I may not have gone where I intended to go, but I think I have ended up where I needed to be.

– Douglas Adams, "The Long Dark Tea-Time of the Soul"

Resilience isn't a single skill. It's a variety of skills and coping mechanisms. To bounce back from bumps in the road as well as failures, you should focus on emphasizing the positive.

– Jean Chatzky

Quotes for All the Feels

When you are feeling **Disrespected**

Be not afraid of greatness. Some are born great, some achieve greatness, and others have greatness thrust upon them.

– William Shakespeare, "Twelfth Night"

And those who were seen dancing were thought to be insane by those who could not hear the music.

– Anonymous
(often misattributed to Friedrich Nietzsche)

I respect everybody. You don't have to earn my respect. You earn my disrespect.

– Charlie Murphy

You have enemies? Good. That means you've stood up for something, sometime in your life.

– Ed Greenwood, "The Code of the Harpers"
(often misattributed to Winston Churchill)

Throughout life people will make you mad, disrespect you and treat you bad. Let God deal with the things they do, cause hate in your heart will consume you too.

– Will Smith

I've learned that people will forget what you said, people will forget what you did, but people will never forget how you made them feel.

– Anonymous
(often misattributed to Maya Angelou)

Don't let people disrespect you. My mom says don't open the door to the devil. Surround yourself with positive people.

– Cuba Gooding Jr.

People aren't either wicked or noble. They're like chef's salads, with good things and bad things chopped and mixed together in a vinaigrette of confusion and conflict.

– Daniel Handler as Lemony Snicket, "The Grim Grotto"

When you are feeling **Frustrated**

Whoever wants to reach a distant goal must take many small steps.

– Helmut Schmidt

If you are going through hell, keep going.

– Anonymous
(often misattributed to Winston Churchill)

There is no road too long to the man who advances deliberately and without undue haste; there are no honors too distant to the man who prepares himself for them with patience.

— Jean de la Bruyere

We are what we repeatedly do. Excellence, then, is not an act, but a habit.

— Will Durant
(often misattributed to Aristotle)

Great works are performed not by strength but by perseverance.

— Samuel Johnson, "Rambler #43"

Life is what happens to you while you're busy making other plans.

— Allen Saunders
(often misattributed to John Lennon)

You have within you, right now, everything you need to deal with whatever the world can throw at you.

— Brian Tracy

Focus on the journey, not the destination. Joy is found not in finishing an activity but in doing it.

— Greg Anderson,
"The 22 Non-Negotiable Laws of Wellness"

When you are feeling
Hateful

Darkness cannot drive out darkness: only light can do that. Hate cannot drive out hate: only love can do that.

– Martin Luther King Jr.

Be kind, for everyone you meet is fighting a harder battle.

– John Watson (paraphrased)
(often misattributed to Plato)

Loving people live in a loving world. Hostile people live in a hostile world. Same world.

– Wayne Dyer

Our judgments when we are pleased and friendly are not the same as when we are pained and hostile.

– Aristotle, "Rhetoric"

Let no man pull you so low as to hate him.

– Martin Luther King Jr.

Constant kindness can accomplish much. As the sun makes ice melt, kindness causes misunderstanding, mistrust, and hostility to evaporate.

– Albert Schweitzer

If we could read the secret history of our enemies we should find in each man's life sorrow and suffering enough to disarm all hostility.

– Henry Wadsworth Longfellow

The secret of happiness is this: let your interests be as wide as possible, and let your reactions to the things and persons that interest you be as far as possible friendly rather than hostile.

– Bertrand Russell, "The Conquest of Happiness"

When you are feeling **Jealous**

You can be the moon and still be jealous of the stars.

— Gary Allan, "Learning to Live with Me"

Some animals are cunning and evil-disposed, as the fox; others, as the dog, are fierce, friendly, and fawning. Some are gentle and easily tamed, as the elephant; some are susceptible of shame, and watchful, as the goose. Some are jealous and fond of ornament, as the peacock.

— Aristotle, "History of Animals"

Never underestimate the power of jealousy and the power of envy to destroy. Never underestimate that.

— Oliver Stone

He that is jealous is not in love.

— Saint Augustine, "Confessions, Book 1" (paraphrased)

An iron is eaten away by rust, so the envious are consumed by their own passion.

– Antisthenes

Jealousy is a mental cancer.

– B.C. Forbes

The jealous are troublesome to others, but a torment to themselves.

– William Penn

Jealousy is all the fun you think they had.

– Erica Jong

When you are feeling **Judgmental**

It's very easy to be judgmental until you know someone's truth.

– Kate Winslet

Be curious, not judgmental.

– Anonymous
(often misattributed to Walt Whitman)

The highest form of ignorance is when you reject something you don't know anything about.

— Wayne Dyer

It is the mark of an educated mind to be able to entertain a thought without accepting it.

— Lowell L. Bennion, "Religion and the Pursuit of Truth" (often misattributed to Aristotle)

You never really understand a person until you consider things from his point of view… Until you climb inside of his skin and walk around in it.

– Harper Lee, "To Kill a Mockingbird" (paraphrased)

If you judge a fish by its ability to climb a tree, it will live its whole life believing that it is stupid.

– Anonymous
(often misattributed to Albert Einstein)

If you judge people, you have no time to love them.

> – Mother Teresa

Courage is what it takes to stand up and speak; courage is also what it takes to sit down and listen.

> – Anonymous
> (often misattributed to Winston Churchill)

When you are feeling **Pessimistic**

Optimism is the faith that leads to achievement. Nothing can be done without hope and confidence.

— Helen Keller, "Optimism"

A pessimist sees the difficulty in every opportunity; an optimist sees the opportunity in every difficulty.

— Bertram Carr (paraphrased)
(often misattributed to Winston Churchill)

Your attitude, not your aptitude, will determine your altitude.

— Zig Ziglar

Most wars are won or lost in our own heads.

— David Goggins,
"Can't Hurt Me: Master Your Mind and Defy the Odds"

It takes no more time to see the good side of life than it takes to see the bad.

– Jimmy Buffett

The meaning of things lies not in the things themselves, but in our attitude towards them.

– Antoine de Saint-Exupéry

If you're not positive energy, you're negative energy.

— Mark Cuban

The greatest discovery of all time is that a person can change his future by merely changing his attitude.

— Oprah Winfrey

When you are feeling **Resentful**

I feel like unforgiveness, bitterness, and resentment, it blocks the flows of God's blessings in life.

– Ja Rule

Resentment is like drinking poison and waiting for the other person to die.

– Bert Ghezzi (paraphrased)
(often misattributed to Saint Augustine and others)

To show resentment at a reproach is to acknowledge that one may have deserved it.

— Tacitus, "The Annals"

The final proof of greatness lies in being able to endure criticism without resentment.

— Elbert Hubbard

Reject your sense of injury and the injury itself disappears.

— Marcus Aurelius, "Meditations"

The trouble with having an open mind, of course, is that people will insist on coming along and trying to put things in it.

— Sir Terry Pratchett, "Diggers"

Our fatigue is often caused not by work, but by worry, frustration, and resentment.

– Dale Carnegie, "How to Stop Worrying and Start Living"

In three words I can sum up everything I've learned about life: it goes on.

– Robert Frost

When you are feeling **Vindictive**

The weak can never forgive. Forgiveness is the attribute of the strong.

— Mahatma Gandhi

It is in the pardoning that we are pardoned.

— Father Esther Bouquerel,
"The Prayer of St. Francis of Assisi Francis of Assisi"

An eye for an eye will only make the whole world blind.

— Mahatma Gandhi

Always forgive your enemies – nothing annoys them so much.

— Percy Colson (paraphrased)
(often misattributed to Oscar Wilde)

A man that studieth revenge keeps his own wounds green.

– Sir Francis Bacon, "Of Revenge"

Sometimes the greatest test is how you quietly handle those who so boldly mishandled you.

– Morgan Richard Oliver

Vindictive

While seeking revenge, dig two graves — one for yourself.

– Douglas Horton

I shall allow no man to belittle my soul by making me hate him.

– Booker T. Washington, "Up From Slavery" (paraphrased)

Quotes for All the Feels

EMPTY FEELINGS

When you are feeling **Apathetic**

Unless someone like you cares a whole awful lot, nothing is going to get better. It's not.

– Theodor Geisel as Dr. Seuss, "The Lorax"

No matter what people tell you, words and ideas can change the world.

– John Keating, played by Robin Williams
"Dead Poets Society"
Directed by Peter Weir
Touchdown Pictures, Walt Disney Company

Is it ignorance or apathy? …Hey, I don't know and I don't care.

– Jimmy Buffett, "I Don't Know & I Don't Care"

Be the change that you wish to see in the world.

– Arleen Lorrance
(often misattributed to Mahatma Gandhi)

I have a very strong feeling that the opposite of love is not hate – it's apathy. It's not giving a damn.

– Leo Buscaglia

You only live once, but if you do it right, once is enough.

– Mae West

We may have found a cure for most evils, but we have found no remedy for the worst of them all, the apathy of human beings.

– Helen Keller, "My Religion"

Apathy can be overcome by enthusiasm, and enthusiasm can only be aroused by two things: first, an ideal, which takes the imagination by storm, and second, a definite intelligible plan for carrying that ideal into practice.

– Arnold J. Toynbee

When you are feeling **Discontented**

Restlessness is discontent and discontent is the first necessity of progress. Show me a thoroughly satisfied man and I will show you a failure.

— Thomas A. Edison

There comes a time when the world gets quiet and the only thing left is your own heart. So you'd better learn the sound of it. Otherwise you'll never understand what it's saying.

— Sarah Dessen, "Just Listen"

If the decisions you make about where you invest your blood, sweat, and tears are not consistent with the person you aspire to be, you'll never become that person.

– Clayton M. Christensen

Choose a job you love, and you will never have to work a day in your life.

– Anonymous
(often misattributed to Confuscius)

Healthy discontent is the prelude to progress.

— Mahatma Gandhi

The one who plants trees, knowing he will never sit in their shade, has at least started to understand the meaning of life.

— Anonymous
(often misattributed to Rabindranath Tagore)

Discontented

Your work is going to fill a large part of your life, and the only way to be truly satisfied is to do what you believe is great work. And the only way to do great work is to love what you do. If you haven't found it yet, keep looking. Don't settle. As with all matters of the heart, you'll know when you find it.

– Steve Jobs

When you are feeling **Disillusioned**

Those who don't believe in magic will never find it.

– Roald Dahl, "The Minpins"

Listen to the mustn'ts, child. Listen to the don'ts. Listen to the shouldn'ts, the impossibles, the won'ts. Listen to the never haves, then listen close to me— Anything can happen, child. Anything can be.

– Shel Silverstein, "Where the Sidewalk Ends"

The challenge of modernity is to live without illusions and without becoming disillusioned.

— Antonio Gramsci

Learn from yesterday, live for today, hope for tomorrow. The important thing is to not stop questioning.

— Albert Einstein

Happiness is when what you think, what you say, and what you do are in harmony.

— Mahatma Gandhi

Hold fast to dreams, for if dreams die life is a broken-winged bird, that cannot fly.

— Langston Hughes, "Dreams"

Nothing can resist the person who smiles at life.

— Pierre Teilhard de Chardin

Everything you can imagine is real.

— Pablo Picasso

When you are feeling **Hopeless**

The greater the obstacle, the more glory in overcoming it.

— Jean-Baptiste Poquelin as Molière, "Amphitryon"

Patience and perseverance have a magical effect before which difficulties disappear and obstacles vanish.

— John Quincy Adams (paraphrased)

Everything is possible. The impossible just takes longer.

— Dan Brown, "Digital Fortress"

All the darkness in the world cannot extinguish the light of a single candle.

— Anonymous
(often misattributed to Francis of Assisi)

You can do anything as long as you have the passion, the drive, the focus, and the support.

– Sabrina Bryan

It is often when night looks darkest, it is often before the fever breaks that one senses the gathering momentum for change, when one feels that resurrection of hope in the midst of despair and apathy.

– Hillary Clinton

What's meant to be will always find a way.

> – Trisha Yearwood, "She's in Love with the Boy"

Nothing is impossible, the word itself says 'I'm possible'!

> – Audrey Hepburn

When you are feeling a sense of **Longing**

The act of longing for something will always be more intense than the requiting of it.

– Gail Godwin, The Finishing School

Feeling and longing are the motive forces behind all human endeavor and human creations.

– Albert Einstein, "Religion and Science"

If some longing goes unmet, don't be astonished. We call that Life.

— Anna Freud

There is a space between man's imagination and man's attainment that may only be transversed by his longing.

— Kahlil Gibran, "Sand and Foam"

This hunger is better than any fullness; this poverty better than all other wealth.

– C.S. Lewis, "The Pilgrim's Regress"

Is there anything better than to be longing for something, when you know it is within reach?

– Greta Garbo

Longing is like the rosy dawn. After the dawn out comes the sun. Longing is followed by the vision of God.

– Sri Ramakrishna

It seems to me we can never give up longing and wishing while we are thoroughly alive. There are certain things we feel to be beautiful and good, and we must hunger after them.

– George Eliot, "The Mill on the Floss"

When you are feeling
Lost

There are years that question, and years that answer.

– Zora Neale Hurston

The two most important days in your life are the day you're born and the day you find out why.

– Anonymous
(often misattributed to Mark Twain)

Not all those who wander are lost.

> – J.R.R. Tolkien, "The Fellowship of the Ring"

Life isn't about finding yourself. Life is about creating yourself.

> – Sydney J. Harris (paraphrased)
> (often misattributed to George Bernard Shaw)

Do not go where the path may lead, go instead where there is no path and leave a trail.

– Ralph Waldo Emerson, "Self-Reliance"

You have brains in your head. You have feet in your shoes. You can steer yourself any direction you choose. You're on your own. And you know what you know. And YOU are the one who'll decide where to go…

– Theodor Geisel as Dr. Seuss, "Oh, the Places You'll Go"

Searching is half the fun: life is much more manageable when thought of as a scavenger hunt as opposed to a surprise party.

– Jimmy Buffett, "A Pirate Looks at Fifty"

Life can only be understood backwards; but it must be lived forwards.

– Soren Kierkegaard

When you are feeling **Nostalgic**

That it will never come again is what makes life sweet.

— Emily Dickinson

Don't cry because it's over, smile because it happened.

— Ludwig Jacobowski (paraphrased)
(often misattributed to Dr. Seuss)

There are no happy endings. Endings are the saddest part, So just give me a happy middle And a very happy start.

— Shel Silverstein, "Every Thing On It"

In the end, just three things matter: How well we have lived. How well we have loved. How well we have learned to let go.

— Jack Kornfield, "Buddha's Little Instruction Book"

Memories warm you up from the inside. But they also tear you apart.

– Haruki Murakami, "Kafka on the Shore"

Sweet is the memory of distant friends! Like the mellow rays of the departing sun, it falls tenderly, yet sadly, on the heart.

– Washington Irving, "The Sketch Book"

I can't go back to yesterday because I was a different person then.

— Lewis Carroll, "Alice in Wonderland"

To live is the rarest thing in the world. Most people exist, that is all.

— Oscar Wilde, "The Soul of Man Under Socialism"

When you are feeling **Sensitive**

We cannot be more sensitive to pleasure without being more sensitive to pain.

– Alan Watts, "The Wisdom of Insecurity"

Some people feel the rain. Others just get wet.

– Roger Miller
(often misattributed to Bob Marley or Bob Dylan)

Tell me I'm clever, tell me I'm kind, tell me I'm talented, tell me I'm cute, tell me I'm sensitive, graceful and wise, tell me I'm perfect – but tell me the truth.

– Shel Silverstein, "Falling Up"

Do not give in too much to feelings. An overly sensitive heart is an unhappy possession on this shaky earth.

– Johann Wolfgang von Goethe, "The Sorrows of Young Werther"

The sensitivity of men to small matters, and their indifference to great ones, indicates a strange inversion.

— Blaise Pascal, "Pensées" (paraphrased)

Wallow too much in sensitivity and you can't deal with life, or the truth.

— Neal Boortz

It is usually the imagination that is wounded first, rather than the heart; it being much more sensitive.

– Henry David Thoreau

I believe that the biggest problem that humanity faces is an ego sensitivity to finding out whether one is right or wrong and identifying what one's strengths and weaknesses are.

– Ray Dalio

When you are feeling **Vulnerable**

Being vulnerable to somebody you love is not a weakness, it's a strength.

– Elisabeth Shue

The best thing to do when you find yourself in a hurting or vulnerable place is to surround yourself with the strongest, finest, most positive people you know.

– Kristin Armstrong

Embrace your vulnerability and celebrate your flaws; it will let you appreciate the world around you and make you more compassionate.

– Masaba Gupta

When we were children, we used to think that when we were grown-up we would no longer be vulnerable. But to grow up is to accept vulnerability… To be alive is to be vulnerable.

– Madeleine L'Engle, "Walking on Water"

Love is not love until love's vulnerable.

– Theodore Roethke, "Words for the Wind"

Vulnerability is the essence of romance. It's the art of being, the willingness to look foolish, the courage to say, 'This is me, and I'm interested in you enough to show you my flaws with the hope that you may embrace me for all that I am but, more important, all that I am not.'

– Ashton Kutcher

A friend is someone who knows all about you and still loves you.

— Elbert Hubbard

Love comes when manipulation stops; when you think more about the other person than about his or her reactions to you. When you dare to reveal yourself fully. When you dare to be vulnerable.

— Joyce Brothers,
"Bursting at the Seams: A Wealth of Wit and Wisdom for, and about, Women"

When you are feeling **Withdrawn**

We are only as strong as we are united, as weak as we are divided.

– J.K. Rowling, "Harry Potter and the Goblet of Fire"

No one can live without relationship. You may withdraw into the mountains, become a monk, a sannyasi, wander off into the desert by yourself, but you are related. You cannot escape from that absolute fact. You cannot exist in isolation.

– Jiddu Krishnamurti

I would rather walk with a friend in the dark, than alone in the light.

— Helen Keller

They say a person needs just three things to be truly happy in this world: someone to love, something to do, and something to hope for.

— Tom Bodett

Quotes for All the Feels

FEARFUL FEELINGS

When you are feeling
Afraid

Everything you've ever wanted is sitting on the other side of fear.

– George Addair

Always do what you are afraid to do.

– Ralph Waldo Emerson, "Heroism"

The only thing we have to fear is fear itself.

— Franklin D. Roosevelt

God, grant me the serenity to accept the things I cannot change, the courage to change the things I can, and the wisdom to know the difference.

— Reinhold Niebuhr

Courage is resistance to fear, mastery of fear, not absence of fear.

— Mark Twain, "Pudd'nhead Wilson's Calendar"

Do the thing you fear to do and keep on doing it... that is the quickest and surest way ever yet discovered to conquer fear.

— Dale Carnegie,
"How to Win Friends and Influence People"

Stay afraid, but do it anyway.

– Carrie Fisher

Do one thing every day that scares you.

– Mary Schmich
(often misattributed to Eleanor Roosevelt)

When you are feeling
Apprehensive

The most difficult thing is the decision to act, the rest is merely tenacity.

– Amelia Earhart

Faith is taking the first step even when you can't see the whole staircase.

– Martin Luther King Jr.

I know how it looks. But just start. Nothing is insurmountable.

— Lin Manuel Miranda

Great people do things before they are ready. They do things before they know they can do it. Doing what you're afraid of, getting out of your comfort zone, taking risks — that's what life is.

— Amy Poehler

You miss 100% of the shots you don't take.

– Wayne Gretzky

Leap, and the net will appear.

– John Burroughs

In the end we only regret the chances we didn't take.

– Lewis Carroll

Have you ever noticed how 'What the hell' is always the right decision to make?

– Terry Johnson, "Insignificance"
(often misattributed to Marilyn Monroe)

When you are feeling **Helpless**

Things do not happen. Things are made to happen.

— John F. Kennedy

If opportunity doesn't knock, build a door.

— Milton Berle

Either you run the day or the day runs you.

– Jim Rohn

I am not a product of my circumstances. I am a product of my decisions.

– Stephen R. Covey,
"The 7 Habits of Highly Effective People"

Opportunities don't happen, you create them.

— Chris Grosser

The question isn't who is going to let me; it's who is going to stop me.

— Ayn Rand, "The Fountainhead" (paraphrased)

The most common way people give up their power is by thinking they don't have any.

— Alice Walker

Never allow a person to tell you no who doesn't have the power to say yes.

— Eleanor Roosevelt

When you are feeling **Inadequate**

It is our choices, Harry, that show what we truly are, far more than our abilities.

– J.K. Rowling, "Harry Potter and the Chamber of Secrets"

I generally find that comparison is the fast track to unhappiness. No one ever compares themselves to someone else and comes out even. Nine times out of ten, we compare ourselves to people who are somehow better than us and end up feeling more inadequate.

– Jack Canfield

No one can make you feel inferior without your consent.

– Eleanor Roosevelt

I am nothing special, of this I am sure. I am a common man with common thoughts and I've led a common life. There are no monuments dedicated to me and my name will soon be forgotten, but I've loved another with all my heart and soul, and to me, this has always been enough.

– Nicholas Sparks, "The Notebook"

I have no special talents. I am only passionately curious.

— Albert Einstein

Never by bullied into silence. Never allow yourself to be made a victim. Accept no one's definition of your life; define yourself.

— Robert Frost

The superior man blames himself. The inferior man blames others.

— Don Shula

To love oneself is the beginning of a lifelong romance.

— Oscar Wilde, "An Ideal Husband"

When you are feeling **Indecisive**

Knowing yourself is the beginning of all wisdom.

– Aristotle (paraphrased)

If you don't know where you're going, any road'll take you there.

– George Harrison, "Any Road"

The risk of a wrong decision is preferable to the terror of indecision.

> — Maimonides, "The Guide for the Perplexed"

Indecision may or may not be my problem.

> — Jimmy Buffett, "Don't-Chu-Know"

More is lost by indecision than wrong decision. Indecision is the thief of opportunity.

– Marcus Tullius Cicero (paraphrased)

Action cures fear. Indecision, postponement, on the other hand, fertilize fear.

– David Joseph Schwartz, "The Magic of Thinking Big"

All we have to decide is what to do with the time that is given us.

— J.R.R. Tolkien, "The Fellowship of the Ring"

It is not in the stars to hold our destiny but in ourselves.

— William Shakespeare, "Julius Caesar" (paraphrased)

When you are feeling **Insecure**

Doubt kills more dreams than failure ever will.

– Suzy Kassem

Confidence comes not from always being right but from not fearing to be wrong.

– Peter T. Mcintyre

Whether you think you can, or you think you can't – you're right.

– Henry Ford

I have self-doubt. I have insecurity. I have fear of failure. I have nights when I show up at the arena and I'm like, 'My back hurts, my feet hurt, my knees hurt. I don't have it. I just want to chill.' We all have self-doubt. You don't deny it, but you also don't capitulate to it. You embrace it.

– Kobe Bryant

Remember that great expectations create great capabilities. If you limit your goals to what you know you can achieve, you are setting the bar way too low.

— Ray Dalio

Confidence is contagious... so is lack of confidence.

— Vince Lombardi

As soon as you trust yourself, you will know how to live.

— Johann Wolfgang von Goethe, "Faust"

If we weren't all crazy we would go insane.

— Jimmy Buffett,
"Changes in Latitudes, Changes in Attitudes"

When you are feeling **Rejected**

I believe that rejection is a blessing because it's the universe's way of telling you that there's something better out there.

— Michelle Phan

You're going to have more rejection than acceptance.

— Barry Mann

The best thing we can do with rejection is to make it a learning experience – rejection is a great teacher.

– Adena Friedman

Rejection is a common occurrence. Learning that early and often will help you build up the tolerance and resistance to keep going and keep trying.

– Kevin Feige

Rejection and I are old friends.

— Michaela Watkins

Every candle that gets lit in the dark room must feel a little rejection from the darkness around it, but the last thing I want from those who hold a different world view to me is to accept me.

— Kirk Cameron

Rejection doesn't always mean I'm not good enough.

— Vincent Rodriguez III

It's not easy. I got lots of rejections when I first started out. If you want to write, you have to believe in yourself and not give up. You have to do your best to practice and get better.

— Rick Riordan

When you are feeling
Self-Conscious

You don't need to be accepted by others. You need to accept yourself.

– Thich Nhat Hanh

Be yourself; everyone else is already taken.

– Anonymous
(often misattributed to Oscar Wilde)

The privilege of a lifetime is to become who you truly are.

— Carl Jung (paraphrased)

You wouldn't worry so much about what others think of you if you realized how seldom they do.

— Olin Miller (paraphrased)
(often misattributed to Eleanor Roosevelt)

Why fit in when you were born to stand out?

– Theodor Geisel as Dr. Seuss

Be who you are and say what you feel, because those who mind don't matter, and those who matter don't mind.

– Bernard M. Baruch
(often misattributed to Dr. Seuss)

To find yourself, think for yourself.

– Socrates (paraphrased)

Most people are other people. Their thoughts are someone else's opinions, their lives a mimicry, their passions a quotation.

– Oscar Wilde, "The Importance of Being Earnest"

When you are feeling
Weak

Nothing in the world can take the place of Persistence. Talent will not; nothing is more common than unsuccessful men with talent. Genius will not; unrewarded genius is almost a proverb. Education will not; the world is full of educated derelicts. The slogan 'Press On' has solved and always will solve the problems of the human race.

– Calvin Coolidge

It's not the will to win that matters—everyone has that. It's the will to prepare to win that matters.

– Paul "Bear" Bryant

The only place success comes before work is in the dictionary.

– Anonymous
(often misattributed to Vince Lombardi or Mark Twain)

He who conquers himself is the mightiest warrior.

— Confucius (paraphrased)

What lies behind us and what lies before us are tiny matters compared to what lies within us.

— Henry Haskins, "Meditations in Wall Street"

Willpower is the key to success. Successful people strive no matter what they feel by applying their will to overcome apathy, doubt or fear.

– Dan Millman, "Path of the Peaceful Warrior"

The most important conversations you'll ever have are the ones you'll have with yourself.

– David Goggins,
"Can't Hurt Me: Master Your Mind and Defy the Odds"

When you are feeling
Worried

Do not anticipate trouble or worry about what may never happen. Keep in the sunlight.

— Benjamin Franklin

Worry often gives a small thing a big shadow.

— Swedish Proverb

Whatever is going to happen will happen, whether we worry or not.

— Ana Monnar

Man is not worried by real problems so much as by his imagined anxieties about real problems.

— Epictetus, "Discourses of Epictetus" (paraphrased)

In every life we have some trouble, but when you worry you make it double. Don't worry. Be happy.

– Bobby McFerrin, "Don't Worry Be Happy"

Instead of worrying about what you cannot control, shift your energy to what you can create.

– Roy Bennett,
"The Light in the Heart: Inspirational Thoughts for Living Your Best Life"

A day of worry is more exhausting than a week of work.

– John Lubbock

Worry does not empty tomorrow of its sorrow. It empties today of its strength.

– Corrie Ten Boom, "Clippings from My Notebook"

When you are feeling **Worthless**

You are enough just as you are.

– Meghan Markle

Have patience with all things, but, first of all with yourself.

– Saint Francis de Sales, "Introduction to the Devout Life"

To be yourself in a world that is constantly trying to make you something else is the greatest accomplishment.

– Ralph Waldo Emerson, "Self-Reliance"

To be nobody but yourself in a world which is doing its best day and night to make you like everybody else means to fight the hardest battle which any human being can fight and never stop fighting.

– E.E Cummings

Today you are You, that is truer than true. There is no one alive who is Youer than You.

— Theodor Geisel as Dr. Seuss, "Happy Birthday to You!"

Promise me you'll always remember: You're braver than you believe, and stronger than you seem, and smarter than you think.

— Christopher Robin, voiced by Brady Bluhm
"Pooh's Grand Adventure: The Search for Christopher Robin"
Directed by Karl Geurs
Walt Disney Television Animation

It matters not what someone is born, but what they grow to be.

— J.K. Rowling, "Harry Potter and the Goblet of Fire"

It is better to fail in originality than to succeed in imitation.

— Herman Melville, "Hawthorne and His Works"

Quotes for All the Feels

SAD FEELINGS

When you are feeling **Disappointed**

We must accept finite disappointment, but never lose infinite hope.

– Martin Luther King Jr.

Some days, doing 'the best we can' may still fall short of what we would like to be able to do, but life isn't perfect – on any front – and doing what we can with what we have is the most we should expect of ourselves or anyone else.

– Fred Rogers, "The World According to Mister Rogers: Important Things to Remember"

That which doesn't kill us makes us stronger.

> – Friedrich Nietzsche, "Twilight of the Idols"

Blessed is he who expects nothing, for he shall never be disappointed.

> – Alexander Pope

Perfection is not attainable. But if we chase perfection we can catch excellence.

— Vince Lombardi

The size of your success is measured by the strength of your desire; the size of your dream; and how you handle disappointment along the way.

— Robert Kiyosaki

When we focus on our gratitude, the tide of disappointment goes out and the tide of love rushes in.

— Kirstin Armstrong

When expectations are too high, sometimes the disappointment is out of proportion.

— Deco

When you are feeling **Embarrassed**

Embarrassment is where growth happens.

– Jaylen Brown

You know what the happiest animal on Earth is? It's a goldfish. You know why? Got a 10-second memory. Be a goldfish.

– Ted Lasso, voiced by Jason Sudeikis
Ted Lasso, "Biscuits" (S1:E2)
Directed by Zach Braff
Universal Television

The rate at which a person can mature is directly proportional to the embarrassment he can tolerate.

— Douglas Engelbart

One person's embarrassment is another person's accountability.

— Tom Price

The best gift you can give yourself is getting over the fear of embarrassment because then you're completely free to try anything.

— Jesse Itzler

If you haven't been amassing embarrassment you've been not taking enough risks in life.

— Lou Sanders

Remembering that I'll be dead soon is the most important tool I've ever encountered to help me make the big choices in life. Because almost everything – all external expectations, all pride, all fear of embarrassment or failure – these things just fall away in the face of death, leaving only what is truly important.

– Steve Jobs

When you are feeling **Heartbroken**

Tis better to have loved and lost than never to have loved at all.

– Alfred Lord Tennyson, "In Memoriam A.H.H."

To be happy you must: let go of what's gone, be grateful for what remains, and look forward to what is coming next.

– Anonymous

Not till we have lost the world, do we begin to find ourselves.

— Henry David Thoreau, "Walden"

When one door of happiness closes, another opens, but often we look so long at the closed door, that we do not see the one that has been opened for us.

— Helen Keller

The world breaks everyone and afterward many are strong at the broken places.

– Ernest Hemingway, "A Farewell to Arms"

The heart was made to be broken.

– Oscar Wilde

It's only after we've lost everything that we're free to do anything.

– Chuck Palahniuk, "Fight Club"

It isn't what you have or who you are or where you are or what you are doing that makes you happy or unhappy. It is what you think about it.

– Dale Carnegie,
"How to Win Friends and Influence People"

When you are feeling **Hurt**

The turning point in the process of growing up is when you discover the core of strength within you that survives all hurt.

— Max Lerner, "The Unfinished Country"

Pain is inevitable. Suffering is optional.

— Haruki Murakami,
"What I Talk About When I Talk About Running"

Truth is everybody is going to hurt you: you just gotta find the ones worth suffering for.

— Bob Marley

Nobody can hurt me without my permission.

— Mahatma Gandhi

No man is hurt but by himself.

— Diogenes of Sinope

Life is pain, highness. Anyone who says differently is selling something.

— The Dread Pirate Roberts, played by Cary Elwes
"The Princess Bride"
Directed by Rob Reiner
Act III Communications

Turn your wounds into wisdom.

– Oprah Winfrey

You don't get to choose if you get hurt in this world…but you do have some say in who hurts you. I like my choices.

– John Green, "The Fault in Our Stars"

When you are feeling **Let Down**

You may not control all the events that happen to you, but you can decide not to be reduced by them.

– Maya Angelou, "Letter to My Daughter"

If you expect nothing from anybody, you're never disappointed.

– Sylvia Plath, "The Bell Jar"

It is easier to forgive an enemy than to forgive a friend.

— William Blake, "Jerusalem"

You were never asking for too much. You were simply just asking the wrong person.

— Bianca Sparacino, "A Gentle Reminder"

There is no disappointment so numbing as someone not showing up, and there is no satisfaction as sweet as having someone make way for you.

— Amy Poehler, "Yes Please"

Trust is like a vase. Once it's broken, though you can fix it, the vase will never be the same again.

— Carol Brady played by Florence Henderson
The Brady Bunch, "Confessions, Confessions" (S2:E12)
Directed by Russ Mayberry
Paramount Television

When someone shows you who they are believe them; the first time.

> – Maya Angelou, "A Song Flung Up to Heaven"

When you're doing good, everybody praises you. But when everything's all gone, a lot of people are nowhere to be found. So you always just believe in yourself, do it yourself and you won't be let down.

> – Ginuwine

When you are feeling
Like a Failure

Never let success get to your head and never let failure get to your heart.

— Drake, "Started from the Bottom"

Our greatest glory is not in never falling, but in rising every time we fall.

— Oliver Goldsmith
(often misattributed to Confucius)

I have not failed. I've just found 10,000 ways that won't work.

– Thomas A. Edison

Failure is success in progress.

– Anonymous
(often misattributed to Albert Einstein)

Discouragement and failure are two of the surest stepping stones to success.

– Dale Carnegie, "How to Win Friends & Influence People"

I've missed more than 9,000 shots in my career. I've lost almost 300 games. 26 times, I've been trusted to take the game-winning shot and missed. I've failed over and over and over again in my life. And that is why I succeed.

– Michael Jordan, "Failure" Commercial for Nike (1997)

Even if you fall on your face you're still moving forward.

— Victor Kiam

Success is not final; failure is not fatal: It is the courage to continue that counts.

— Anonymous
(often misattributed to Winston Churchill)

When you are feeling
Lonely

The only way to have a friend is to be one.

– Ralph Waldo Emerson, "Friendship"

You can't stay in your corner of the Forest waiting for others to come to you. You have to go to them sometimes.

– A.A. Milne, "Winnie-the-Pooh"

Lonely

Everyone, at some point in their lives, wakes up in the middle of the night with the feeling that they are all alone in the world, and that nobody loves them now and that nobody will ever love them, and that they will never have a decent night's sleep again and will spend their lives wandering blearily around a loveless landscape, hoping desperately that their circumstances will improve, but suspecting, in their heart of hearts, that they will remain unloved forever. The best thing to do in these circumstances is to wake somebody else up, so that they can feel this way, too.

– Daniel Handler as Lemony Snicket, "The Bad Beginning"

You cannot do kindness too soon, for you never know how soon it will be too late.

– Ralph Waldo Emerson

Absence is to love what wind is to fire; it extinguishes the small, it inflames the great.

– Roger de Bussy-Rabutin, "Histoire Amoureuse des Gaules"

Lonely

There's a difference between solitude and loneliness.

— Maggie Smith

The friend who can be silent with us in a moment of despair or confusion, who can stay with us in an hour of grief and bereavement, who can tolerate not knowing… not healing, not curing… that is a friend who cares.

— Henri Nouwen, "Out of Solitude"

When you are feeling **Regretful**

Forgiveness of oneself is the hardest of all the forgivenesses.

– Joan Baez

I'd rather regret the things I've done than regret the things I haven't done.

– Lucille Ball

For all the sad words of tongue and pen, the saddest are these, 'It might have been.'

— John Greenleaf Whittier, "Maud Muller"

Anyone who has never made a mistake has never tried anything new.

— Anonymous
(often misattributed to Albert Einstein)

A life spent making mistakes is not only more honorable, but more useful than a life spent doing nothing.

– George Bernard Shaw, "Heartbreak House"

When you do something that maybe wasn't the best thing to do at the time, you don't want to hold onto those feelings of guilt, shame, or embarrassment, as much as you'd like to learn from them.

– Andrew W.K.

We should regret our mistakes and learn from them, but never carry them forward into the future with us.

— Lucy Maud Montgomery, "Anne of Avonlea"

Make the most of your regrets; never smother your sorrow, but tend and cherish it till it comes to have a separate and integral interest. To regret deeply is to live afresh.

— Henry David Thoreau

When you are feeling
Sad

Happiness is not having what you want, but wanting what you have.

– Rabbi Hyman Schachtel, "The Real Enjoyment of Living"

The more you practice the art of thankfulness, the more you have to be thankful for.

– Norman Vincent Peale

You cannot protect yourself from sadness without protecting yourself from happiness.

– Jonathan Safran Foer, "Everything Is Illuminated"

Happiness is not a destination, it's a journey. Happiness is not tomorrow, it is now. Happiness is not a dependency, it is a decision. Happiness is what you are, not what you have.

– Zig Ziglar

The happiness of your life depends upon the quality of your thoughts.

– Marcus Aurelius, "Meditations"

Folks are usually about as happy as they make their minds up to be.

– Anonymous
(often misattributed to Abraham Lincoln)

Happiness is not something ready made. It comes from your own actions.

— Dalai Lama XIV

You can't be happy unless you're unhappy sometimes.

— Lauren Oliver, "Delirium"

Quotes for All the Feels

STRESSED FEELINGS

When you are feeling **Anxious**

Nothing diminishes anxiety faster than action.

– Walter Anderson

Our anxiety does not empty tomorrow of its sorrows, but only empties today of its strengths.

– Alexander McLaren (paraphrased)
(often misattributed to C.H. Spurgeon)

Anxiety is like a rocking chair. It gives you something to do, but it doesn't get you very far.

– Jodi Picoult, "Sing You Home"

Never let the future disturb you. You will meet it, if you have to, with the same weapons of reason which today arm you against the present.

– Marcus Aurelius, "Meditations"

I get nervous when I don't get nervous. If I'm nervous, I know I'm going to have a good show.

– Beyonce Knowles

I've learned over the years that if you start thinking about the race, it stresses you out a little bit. I just try to relax and think about video games, what I'm gonna do after the race, what I'm gonna do just to chill. Stuff like that to relax a little before the race.

– Usain Bolt

I'm at my best when I'm nervous, scared. I feel like I'm on the edge, that's when I perform better.

– Georges St-Pierre

You don't have to control your thoughts. You just have to stop letting them control you.

– Dan Millman

When you are feeling **Burned Out**

You will burn and you will burn out; you will be healed and come back again.

– Fyodor Dostoevsky, "The Brothers Karamazov"

Almost everything will work again if you unplug it for a few minutes, including you.

– Anne Lamott

Sometimes the most important thing in a whole day is the rest taken between two deep breaths.

— Etty Hillesum

Just because you take breaks doesn't mean you're broken.

— Curtis Tyrone Jones

Relaxing brings weakness, when done by a muscle; but brings strength, when done by a person.

— Mokokoma Mokohonoana

Smile, breath, and go slowly.

— Thich Nhat Hanh

Everything goes in cycles, to a degree.

– Herb Brooks

Time you enjoy wasting is not wasted time.

– Marthe Troly-Curtin, "Phrynette Married"
(often misattributed to Bertrand Russell)

When you are feeling **Confused**

Truth is ever to be found in simplicity, and not in the multiplicity and confusion of things.

– Isaac Newton, "Rules for methodizing the Apocalypse"

Truth emerges more readily from error than from confusion.

– Sir Francis Bacon, "Of Truth"

None but ourselves can free our minds.

— Bob Marley, "Redemption Song"

Human life itself may be almost pure chaos, but the work of the artist is to take these handfuls of confusion and disparate things, things that seem to be irreconcilable, and put them together in a frame to give them some kind of shape and meaning.

— Katherine Anne Porter

We're taught to be ashamed of confusion, anger, fear and sadness, and to me they're of equal value to happiness, excitement and inspiration.

— Alanis Morissette

The unexamined life is not worth living.

— Socrates, "Plato's Apology"

Confusion of goals and perfection of means seems, in my opinion, to characterize our age.

— Albert Einstein

Mixed feelings, like mixed drinks, are a confusion to the soul.

— George Carlin

Quotes for All the Feels

When you are feeling **Impatient**

He that can have patience can have what he will.

— Benjamin Franklin, "Poor Richard's Almanack"

Patience is bitter, but its fruit is sweet.

— John Chardin,
"Voyages en Perse et autres lieux de l'Orient"
(often misattributed to Jean-Jacques Rousseau)

With love and patience, nothing is impossible.

— Daisaku Ikeda, "For Today & Tomorrow"

Have patience. All things are difficult before they become easy.

— Anonymous
(often misattributed to Thomas Fuller)

Good character is not formed in a week or a month. It is created little by little, day by day. Protracted and patient effort is needed to develop good character.

— Heraclitus, "On Nature"

A man who is a master of patience is master of everything else.

— George Savile,
"Political, Moral, and Miscellaneous Reflections"

It is easier to find men who will volunteer to die, than to find those who are willing to endure pain with patience.

— Julius Caesar, "Commentaries on the Gallic War"

Only those who have patience to do simple things perfectly ever acquire the skill to do difficult things easily.

— James J. Corbett

When you are feeling **Overwhelmed**

Do what you can, with what you have, where you are.

— Theodore Roosevelt

All great changes are preceded by chaos.

— Deepak Chopra

Things which matter most must not be at the mercy of things which matter least.

— Johann Wolfgang von Goethe

It's not the load that breaks you down, it's the way you carry it.

— Lou Holtz

Let everything happen to you: Beauty and terror. Just keep going. No feeling is final.

– Ranier Maria Rilke, "Book of Hours: Love Poems to God"

If you choose not to decide, you still have made a choice.

– Rush, "Freewill"

I promise you nothing is as chaotic as it seems. Nothing is worth diminishing your health. Nothing is worth poisoning yourself into stress, anxiety, and fear.

– Steve Maraboli

Being overwhelmed means that your life or work is overpowering you. Regain control by clarifying your intentions, setting realistic expectations and focusing on your next step.

– Daphne Michaels

When you are feeling
Stressed

The greatest weapon against stress is our ability to choose one thought over another.

– William James

In times of great stress or adversity, it's always best to keep busy, to plow your anger and your energy into something positive.

– Lee Iacocca

God will never give you anything you can't handle, so don't stress.

— Kelly Clarkson

Being in control of your life and having realistic expectations about your day-to-day challenges are the keys to stress management, which is perhaps the most important ingredient to living a happy, healthy and rewarding life.

— Marilu Henner

Adopting the right attitude can convert a negative stress into a positive one.

— Hans Selye

The truth is that there is no actual stress or anxiety in the world; it's your thoughts that create these false beliefs. You can't package stress, touch it, or see it. There are only people engaged in stressful thinking.

— Wayne Dyer

Stress is a downward spiral, and you can only overcome it with a positive perspective.

— Jen Lilley

My key to dealing with stress is simple: just stay cool and stay focused.

— Ashton Eaton

When you are feeling
Under Pressure

Enjoy the pressure. Enjoy the stress. Enjoy being uncomfortable. And don't shy away from it, embrace it.

– Gary Woodland

Pressure Makes Diamonds.

– George S. Patton, Jr.

We delight in the beauty of the butterfly, but rarely admit the changes it has gone through to achieve that beauty.

– Maya Angelou

If you are working on something that you really care about, you don't have to be pushed. The vision pulls you.

– Steve Jobs

Quotes for All the Feels

TIRED FEELINGS

Quotes for All the Feels

When you are feeling **Bored**

He who seeks rest finds boredom. He who seeks work finds rest.

– Dylan Thomas

Boredom is your imagination calling to you.

– Sherry Turkle, "Reclaiming Conversation: The Power of Talk in a Digital Age"

There's no excuse to be bored. Sad, yes. Angry, yes. Depressed, yes. Crazy, yes. But there's no excuse for boredom, ever.

– Viggo Mortensen

Boredom always precedes a period of great creativity.

– Robert M. Pirsig,
"Zen and the Art of Motorcycle Maintenance"

The life of the creative man is led, directed and controlled by boredom. Avoiding boredom is one of our most important purposes.

— Susan Sontag

The cure for boredom is curiosity. There is no cure for curiosity.

— Ellen Parr
(often misattributed to Dorothy Parker)

Boredom is the feeling that everything is a waste of time; serenity, that nothing is.

– Thomas Szasz, "The Myth of the Mental Illness"

Boredom or discontent is useful to me when I acknowledge it and see clearly my assumption that there's something else I would rather be doing.

– Hugh Prather, "Notes to Myself"

When you are feeling **Exhausted**

Don't stop when you're tired. Stop when you're done.

— David Goggins

If you get tired, learn to rest, not to quit.

— Banksy

Pain is temporary. Quitting lasts forever.

> – Lance Armstrong, "It's Not About the Bike"

The battles that count aren't the ones for gold medals. The struggles within yourself—the invisible, inevitable battles inside all of us—that's where it's at.

> – Jesse Owens,
> "Blackthink: My Life as Black Man and White Man"

You just can't beat the person who never gives up.

— Babe Ruth

I've got a great ambition to die of exhaustion rather than boredom.

— Thomas Carlyle

One, remember to look up at the stars and not down at your feet. Two, never give up work. Work gives you meaning and purpose.

– Stephen Hawking

If you want to build a ship, don't drum up people to collect wood and don't assign them tasks and work, but rather teach them to long for the endless immensity of the sea.

– Antoine de Saint-Exupéry, "Citadelle" (paraphrased)

When you are feeling
Stagnant

Life is like riding a bicycle. To keep your balance you must keep moving.

– Albert Einstein

If you can't fly then run, if you can't run then walk, if you can't walk then crawl, but whatever you do you have to keep moving forward.

– Martin Luther King Jr.

Well done is better than well said.

— Benjamin Franklin

The only way to get a thing done is to start to do it, then keep on doing it, and finally you'll finish it.

— Langston Hughes, "The Big Sea"

One of the differences between some successful and unsuccessful people is that one group is full of doers, while the other is full of wishers.

— Edmond Mbiaka

Live as if you were to die tomorrow. Learn as if you were to live forever.

— Anonymous
(often misattributed to Mahatma Gandhi)

Get a good idea and stay with it. Dog it, and work at it until it's done right.

> – Don Eddy, interviewing Walt Disney

We're either getting better or we're getting worse.

> – David Goggins

When you are feeling
Stuck

The only way through is through.

— Robert Frost, "A Servant to Servants" (paraphrased)

Nothing changes if nothing changes.

— Theo Von

If you really want to do something, you'll find a way. If you don't, you'll find an excuse.

– Jim Rohn

Just Keep Swimming.

– Dory, voiced by Ellen DeGeneres
"Finding Nemo"
Directed by Andrew Stanton
Pixar Animation Studios

Nothing that's worthwhile is ever easy. Remember that.

– Nicholas Sparks, "Message in a Bottle"

Courage doesn't always roar. Sometimes courage is a quiet voice at the end of the day saying, "I will try again tomorrow."

– Mary Anne Radmacher, "Courage Doesn't Always Roar"

You have your way. I have my way. As for the right way, the correct way, and the only way, it does not exist.

– Friedrich Nietzsche

Let your joy be in your journey – not in some distant goal.

– Tim Cook

When you are having **Trouble Starting**

A year from now you will wish you had started today.

— Karen Lamb

The secret of getting ahead is getting started.

— Anonymous
(often misattributed to Mark Twain)

You cannot plow a field by turning it over in your mind. To begin, begin.

— Gordon B. Hinckley

We all need small sparks, small accomplishments in our lives to fuel the big ones... Because it's the small sparks, which start small fires, that eventually build enough heat to burn the whole ... forest down.

— David Goggins,
"Can't Hurt Me: Master Your Mind and Defy the Odds"

How wonderful it is that nobody need wait a single moment before starting to improve the world.

> – Anne Frank, "Tales from the Secret Annex"

It is never too late to be what you might have been.

> – Adelaide Anne Procter (paraphrased)
> (often misattributed to George Eliot)

Do not wait; the time will never be "just right." Start where you stand, and work with whatever tools you may have at your command.

> – Napoleon Hill, "Think and Grow Rich"

People who think too much before they act don't act too much.

> – Jimmy Buffett

When you are feeling
Unfocused

Concentrate all your thoughts upon the work at hand. The sun's rays do not burn until brought to a focus.

– Alexander Graham Bell

At the end of the day, you can't control the results; you can only control your effort level and your focus.

– Ben Zobrist

The joy we feel has little to do with the circumstances of our lives and everything to do with the focus of our lives.

– Russell M. Nelson

That's been one of my mantras – focus and simplicity. Simple can be harder than complex. You have to work hard to get your thinking clean to make it simple. But it's worth it in the end because once you get there, you can move mountains.

– Steve Jobs

It is during our darkest moments that we must focus to see the light.

— Aristotle Onassis

You can't depend on your eyes when your imagination is out of focus.

— Mark Twain,
"A Connecticut Yankee in King Arthur's Court"

Realize deeply that the present moment is all you ever have. Make the Now the primary focus of your life.

— Eckhart Tolle, "The Power of Now"

Try not to be a man of success. Rather become a man of value.

— Albert Einstein

When you are feeling **Uninspired**

Inspiration does exist, but it must find you working.

— Pablo Picasso

Show up, show up, show up, and after a while the muse shows up, too.

— Isabel Allende

Somewhere, something incredible is waiting to be known.

> – Sharon Begley from an interview with Carl Sagan

If you can dream it, you can do it.

> – Disney Imagineer Tom Fitzgerald
> (often misattributed to Walt Disney)

Someone's sitting in the shade today because someone planted a tree a long time ago.

— Warren Buffet

Tell me, what is it you plan to do with your one wild and precious life?

— Mary Oliver, "House of Light"

We all die. The goal isn't to live forever, the goal is to create something that will.

— Chuck Palahniuk, "Diary"

Twenty years from now you will be more disappointed by the things that you didn't do than by the ones you did do. So throw off the bowlines. Sail away from the safe harbor. Catch the trade winds in your sails. Explore. Dream. Discover.

— H. Jackson Brown Jr., "P.S. I Love You"

When you are feeling **Unmotivated**

Some people want it to happen, some wish it would happen, others make it happen.

— Michael Jordan

Opportunity is missed by most people because it is dressed in overalls and looks like work.

— Anonymous
(often misattributed to Thomas A. Edison)

Hustle beats talent when talent doesn't hustle.

— Ross Simmonds

I'm a great believer in luck, and I find the harder I work the more I have of it.

— Coleman Cox
(often misattributed to Thomas Jefferson)

Be miserable. Or motivate yourself. Whatever has to be done, it's always your choice.

– Wayne Dyer

Victory is celebrated in the light, but it is won in the darkness.

– Valya Harkonen, played by Emily Watson
Dune: Prophecy, "The Hidden Hand" (S1:E1)
Directed by Anna Foerster
Warner Bros. Television

The ticket to victory often comes down to bringing your very best when you feel your worst.

– David Goggins,
"Can't Hurt Me: Master Your Mind and Defy the Odds"

Don't say you don't have enough time. You have exactly the same number of hours per day that were given to Helen Keller, Pasteur, Michaelangelo, Mother Teresa, Leonardo Da Vinci, Thomas Jefferson, and Albert Einstein.

– H. Jackson Brown Jr.

Quotes for All the Feels

ACKNOWLEDGEMENTS

Special thanks to my wife, Suzanne, for support with editing and cover design.

AUTHOR INDEX

Adams, Douglas, 35
Adams, John Quincy, 82
Addair, George, 110
Allan, Gary, 48
Allende, Isabel, 246
Anderson, Greg, 43
Anderson, Walter, 194
Angelou, Maya, 20, 25, 30, 38, 172, 175, 219
Anonymous, 10, 13, 14, 19, 36, 38, 40, 52, 54, 55, 75, 76, 83, 90, 138, 143, 164, 177, 179, 185, 190, 207, 232, 238, 250
Antisthenes, 50
Aristotle, 10, 12, 41, 45, 48, 53, 126, 244
Armstrong, Kirstin, 159
Armstrong, Lance, 227
Aurelius, Marcus, 14, 62, 190, 195
Bacon, Sir Francis, 66, 202
Baez, Joan, 184
Ball, Lucille, 184
Banksy, 226

Baruch, Bernard M., 140
Begley, Sharon, 247
Bell, Alexander Graham, 242
Bennett, Roy, 148
Bennion, Lowell L., 53
Berle, Milton, 118
Blake, William, 173
Bodett, Tom, 107
Bolt, Usain, 196
Boom, Corrie Ten, 149
Boortz, Neal, 100
Bouquerel, Father Esther, 64
Brady, Carol, 174
Bridges, Jeff, 29
Brooks, Herb, 201
Brothers, Joyce, 105
Brown Jr., H. Jackson, 249, 253
Brown, Dan, 83
Brown, Jaylen, 160
Bryan, Sabrina, 84
Bryant, Kobe, 131
Bryant, Paul, 143
Buddhaghoṣa, 13

Buffet, Warren, 248
Buffett, Jimmy, 23, 58, 71, 93, 127, 133, 241
Burdette, Robert J., 21
Burroughs, John, 116
Buscaglia, Leo, 72
Caesar, Julius, 129, 209
Cameron, Kirk, 136
Canfield, Jack, 122
Carlin, George, 205
Carlyle, Thomas, 228
Carnegie, Dale, 63, 112, 167, 178
Carr, Bertram, 56
Carroll, Lewis, 97, 117
Chardin, John, 206
Chatzky, Jean, 35
Chopra, Deepak, 210
Christensen, Clayton M., 75
Cicero, Marcus Tullius, 128
Clarkson, Kelly, 215
Clinton, Hillary, 84
Colbert, Stephen, 28
Colson, Percy, 65
Confucius, 144, 176
Cook, Tim, 237
Coolidge, Calvin, 142
Corbett, James J., 209

Covey, Stephen R., 119
Cox, Coleman, 251
Cuban, Mark, 59
Cummings, E.E, 151
Dahl, Roald, 78
Dalio, Ray, 101, 132
de Bussy-Rabutin, Roger, 182
de Chardin, Pierre Teilhard, 81
de la Bruyere, Jean, 41
de Saint-Exupéry, Antoine, 58, 229
de Sales, Saint Francis, 150
Deco, 159
Dessen, Sarah, 74
Dickinson, Emily, 94
Dory, 235
Dostoevsky, Fyodor, 198
Douglass, Frederick, 34
Drake, 176
Dugan, Jimmy, 33
Dumbledore, 7
Durant, Will, 41
Dyer, Wayne, 45, 53, 216, 252
Earhart, Amelia, 114
Eaton, Ashton, 217
Eddy, Don, 233

Edison, Thomas A., 74, 177, 250
Einstein, Albert, 19, 54, 79, 86, 124, 177, 185, 205, 230, 245, 253
Eliot, George, 89, 240
Emerson, Ralph Waldo, 14, 92, 110, 151, 180, 182
Emperor, The, 34
Engelbart, Douglas, 161
Epictetus, 147
Feige, Kevin, 135
Fisher, Carrie, 113
Fitzgerald, Tom, 247
Foer, Jonathan Safran, 189
Forbes, B.C., 50
Ford, Henry, 32, 131
Frank, Anne, 240
Franklin, Benjamin, 15, 146, 206, 231
Freud, Anna, 87
Freud, Sigmund, 32
Friedman, Adena, 135
Frost, Robert, 63, 124, 234
Gandhi, Mahatma, 64, 65, 71, 76, 80, 169, 232
Garbo, Greta, 88
Geisel, Theodor, 70, 92, 140, 152
Gervais, Ricky, 29
Ghezzi, Bert, 60
Gibran, Kahlil, 87
Ginsburg, Ruth Bader, 16
Ginuwine, 175
Godwin, Gail, 86
Goggins, David, 57, 145, 226, 233, 239, 253
Goldsmith, Oliver, 176
Gooding Jr., Cuba, 39
Gramsci, Antonio, 79
Green, John, 171, 185
Greenwood, Ed, 37
Gretzky, Wayne, 116
Grosser, Chris, 120
Gupta, Masaba, 103
Handler, Daniel, 39, 181
Hanh, Thich Nhat, 138, 200
Hanks, Tom, 33
Harkonen, Valya, 252
Harris, Sydney J., 91
Harrison, George, 126
Haskins, Henry, 144
Hawking, Stephen, 23, 229
Hemingway, Ernest, 166
Henner, Marilu, 215

Hepburn, Audrey, 85
Heraclitus, 208
Hill, Napoleon, 241
Hillesum, Etty, 199
Hinckley, Gordon B., 239
Holtz, Lou, 211
Horton, Douglas, 67
Hubbard, Elbert, 61, 105
Hughes, Langston, 80, 231
Hurston, Zora Neale, 90
Iacocca, Lee, 214
Ikeda, Daisaku, 207
Irving, Washington, 96
Itzler, Jesse, 162
Ja Rule, 60
Jacobowski, Ludwig, 94
James, Lebron, 26
James, William, 214
Jobs, Steve, 77, 163, 219, 243
Johnson, Samuel, 42
Johnson, Terry, 117
Jones, Curtis Tyrone, 199
Jong, Erica, 51
Jordan, Michael, 178, 250
Jung, Carl, 139
Kassem, Suzy, 130
Keating, John, 70
Keller, Helen, 56, 73, 107, 165
Kennedy, John F., 118
Kenny, Elizabeth, 15
Kiam, Victor, 179
Kierkegaard, Soren, 93
King Jr., Martin Luther, 22, 44, 46, 114, 156, 230
Kiyosaki, Robert, 158
Knowles, Beyonce, 196
Kornfield, Jack, 95
Krishnamurti, Jiddu, 106
Kutcher, Ashton, 104
L'Engle, Madeleine, 103
Lama XIV, Dalai, 191
Lamb, Karen, 238
Lamott, Anne, 198
Lasso, Ted, 160
Lee, Harper, 54
Lerner, Max, 168
Lewis, C.S., 88
Lilley, Jen, 217
Lombardi, Vince, 132, 143, 158
Longfellow, Henry Wadsworth, 47
Lorrance, Arleen, 71
Lubbock, John, 149
Maimonides, 127
Mann, Barry, 134

Maraboli, Steve, 213
Mark Twain, 244
Markle, Meghan, 150
Marley, Bob, 98, 169, 203
Mattis, Jim, 30
Mbiaka, Edmond, 232
McFerrin, Bobby, 148
Mcintyre, Peter T., 130
McLaren, Alexander, 194
Mead, Margaret, 31
Melville, Herman, 153
Michaels, Daphne, 213
Miller, Olin, 139
Miller, Roger, 98
Millman, Dan, 22, 145, 197
Milne, A.A., 180
Milton, John, 16
Miranda, Lin Manuel, 115
Mokohonoana, Mokokoma, 200
Molière, 82
Monnar, Ana, 147
Montgomery, Lucy Maud, 187
Morissette, Alanis, 204
Morita, Pat, 34
Mortensen, Viggo, 223
Mother Teresa, 55, 253
Murakami, Haruki, 96, 168
Murphy, Charlie, 37
Nelson, Russell M., 243
Newton, Isaac, 202
Niebuhr, Reinhold, 111
Nietzsche, Friedrich, 36, 157, 237
Nin, Anais, 17
Nouwen, Henri, 183
Oliver, Lauren, 191
Oliver, Mary, 248
Oliver, Morgan Richard, 66
Onassis, Aristotle, 244
Owens, Jesse, 227
Palahniuk, Chuck, 167, 249
Parr, Ellen, 224
Parton, Dolly, 18
Pascal, Blaise, 100
Patton, George S., 31, 218
Peale, Norman Vincent, 27, 188
Penn, William, 51
Phan, Michelle, 134
Picasso, Pablo, 81, 246
Picoult, Jodi, 195
Pirsig, Robert M., 223
Plath, Sylvia, 172

Poehler, Amy, 115, 174
Pope, Alexander, 157
Poquelin, Jean-Baptiste, 82
Porter, Katherine Anne, 203
Powell, Colin, 12
Pratchett, Sir Terry, 62
Prather, Hugh, 225
Price, Tom, 161
Procter, Adelaide Anne, 240
Radmacher, Mary Anne, 236
Ramakrishna, Sri, 89
Rand, Ayn, 120
Rilke, Ranier Maria, 212
Riordan, Rick, 137
Roberts, The Dread Pirate, 170
Robin, Christopher, 152
Rodriguez III, Vincent, 137
Roethke, Theodore, 104
Rogers, Fred, 156
Rohn, Jim, 119, 235
Roosevelt, Eleanor, 19, 27, 113, 121, 123, 139
Roosevelt, Franklin D., 111
Roosevelt, Teddy, 21
Roosevelt, Theodore, 24, 210
Rowling, J.K., 106, 122, 153
Rush, 212
Russell, Bertrand, 47, 201
Ruth, Babe, 228
Saint Augustine, 49, 60
Sanders, Lou, 162
Saunders, Allen, 42
Savile, George, 208
Schachtel, Rabbi Hyman, 188
Schmich, Mary, 113
Schmidt, Helmut, 40
Schuller, Robert H, 20
Schwartz, David Joseph, 128
Schweitzer, Albert, 46
Selye, Hans, 216
Seneca, Lucius Annaeus, 33
Seuss, Dr., 70, 92, 94, 140, 152
Shakespeare, William, 18, 36, 129
Shaw, George Bernard, 91, 186
Shue, Elisabeth, 102

Shula, Don, 125
Silverstein, Shel, 78, 95, 99
Simmonds, Ross, 251
Sinope, Diogenes of, 170
Smith, Maggie, 183
Smith, Will, 38
Snicket, Lemony, 39, 181
Socrates, 141, 204
Sontag, Susan, 224
Sparacino, Bianca, 173
Sparks, Nicholas, 123, 236
Stone, Oliver, 49
St-Pierre, Georges, 197
Swedish Proverb, 146
Szasz, Thomas, 225
Tacitus, 61
Tennyson, Alfred Lord, 164
Thomas, Dylan, 222
Thoreau, Henry David, 101, 165, 187
Tolkien, J.R.R., 91, 129
Tolle, Eckhart, 245
Tolstoy, Leo, 17
Toynbee, Arnold J., 73
Tracy, Brian, 43
Troly-Curtin, Marthe, 201
Turkle, Sherry, 222
Twain, Mark, 10, 13, 21, 25, 90, 112, 143, 238, 244
Von, Theo, 234
W.K., Andrew, 186
Walker, Alice, 121
Washington, Booker T., 67
Watkins, Michaela, 136
Watson, John, 44
Watts, Alan, 98
West, Mae, 72
Whittier, John Greenleaf, 185
Wilde, Oscar, 65, 97, 125, 138, 141, 166
Winfrey, Oprah, 59, 171
Winslet, Kate, 52
Wolfgang von Goethe, Johann, 99, 133, 211
Wooden, John, 26
Woodland, Gary, 218
Yearwood, Trisha, 85
Ziglar, Zig, 57, 189
Zobrist, Ben, 242

ABOUT THE AUTHOR

Shawn Cornelius has spent over 30 years as a management consultant, IT executive, husband, and father. As a management consultant at Andersen Consulting / Accenture and Rosetta / SapientRazorfish, Shawn has developed a deep passion for the consulting culture of stewardship and teaching. Shawn also served on the Board of Directors for The Centers for Families and Children, a non-profit focused on helping families overcome the barriers of poverty.

Outside of work and philanthropy, Shawn enjoys spending time with his wife, three children, and three grandchildren, who keep him young with their fresh perspectives on the world. As time permits, Shawn attempts (poorly) to continue playing soccer.

This is the third book Shawn has published – one dedicated to each of his children and gifted as a college graduation gift. You can find Shawn's books anywhere books are sold:

- 150 Things You Need to Know Now That You're a Grownup
- The Pre-Med that Could
- Quotes for All the Feels